Kinky Cupcakes

Kinky Cupcakes

Joanna Farrow

spruce

An Hachette UK Company
First published in Great Britain in 2010 by Spruce
a division of Octopus Publishing Group Ltd
Endeavour House, 189 Shaftesbury Avenue,
London, WC2H 8JY
www.octopusbooks.co.uk

Copyright © Octopus Publishing Group Ltd 2010

ISBN 13: 978-1-84601-361-4

A CIP catalogue record for this book is available
from the British Library.

Printed and bound in China

10 9 8 7 6 5 4 3 2 1

Contents

Introduction

The cupcake revolution has been gathering pace for some time now, capturing the imagination of cooks everywhere. *Kinky Cupcakes* comes at a good moment to provide an exciting, artistic and creative new twist on the theme. Here is your chance to create a range of sexy, fun, quirky cakes that are perfect for a variety of occasions from birthdays to girls' nights, and from hen parties to Valentine's Day. Or, on a more intimate level, you could use some of these cute and coquettish creations to entice your partner...

You might want to make a whole batch of one design, or mix and match a few of your favourite decorations within each batch of cakes. Some of the distinctive designs are simple to create but most require a little time, patience and creative input to achieve stylish, rewarding results. These are cakes to become engrossed in, enjoy and nurture to your heart's content.

Buying supplies

A good cake decorating shop will stock all the decorating ingredients and tools you can't buy in the supermarket. Otherwise, check out the Internet for mail-order suppliers.

Check through each recipe before you start. Some include decorations that require overnight setting before assembling, others might need a food colouring or cutter that you'll need to buy.

Choosing cupcake cases

In all the kinky cake designs in this book, the cupcake cases are as much a part of the overall look as the decoration, and the right colour or style will really help to set off the cakes. Most supermarkets sell only plain cupcake cases but there are plenty of stunning designs available from other outlets. Bear in mind that they vary considerably in size, ranging from cute little baby cases to giant muffin cases. The size of your cases will obviously determine the number of cakes you get out of each recipe.

Tips for making and storing cupcakes

As a guide, fill the cupcake cases no more than two-thirds full with cake mixture before baking so the sponge has space to rise as it bakes. If under-filled they won't look effective, if over-filled the mixture will spill out as it cooks. Cook the cakes in the centre of a preheated oven. If the cupcakes fill more than one tray, bake in two separate batches, rather than placing one tray at the top of the oven and the other at the bottom, then rotating the trays halfway through cooking. This will result in perfect cakes every time.

Cupcakes are best served freshly baked. If you don't have time to bake and decorate in the same session, keep the undecorated cakes in an airtight container for up to 24 hours. If storing for longer, it is better to freeze them,

then thaw for several hours at room temperature before decorating.

Once decorated, store cupcakes in a cool place until you eat them, especially if they contain chocolate ganache. Don't put them in the refrigerator, however, or toppings such as ganache and cream cheese frosting will become too hard.

Basic Recipes

Vanilla Cupcakes

1 vanilla pod, or 2 teaspoons vanilla extract
125 g (4 oz) caster sugar
125 g (4 oz) lightly salted butter, softened
2 eggs
1 tablespoon milk
150 g (5 oz) self-raising flour
(Makes 10)

1) Line 10 cups of a muffin tray with paper cupcake cases and preheat the oven to 180°C/350°F/Gas Mark 4.

2) Split the vanilla pod lengthways, if using, and scrape out the seeds with the tip of a knife. Put in a mixing bowl with a spoonful of the sugar and mash together until the seeds are evenly distributed. Add the remaining sugar and cake ingredients and beat with a hand-held electric whisk until pale and creamy. Alternatively, simply whisk the vanilla extract with the remaining ingredients.

3) Divide the mixture among the cupcake cases and bake in the oven for about 25 minutes until risen and just firm. Transfer to a wire rack to cool.

Cherry Cupcakes

Make *Vanilla Cupcakes*, using 1 teaspoon of almond extract instead of the vanilla and 50 g (2 oz) of ground almonds to replace 25 g (1 oz) of the flour. Stir in 100 g (3½ oz) of chopped glacé cherries before baking.

Rich Chocolate Cupcakes

75 g (3 oz) cocoa powder
225 ml (7½ fl oz) boiling water
125 g (4 oz) lightly salted butter, softened
275 g (9 oz) light muscovado sugar
2 eggs
200 g (7 oz) plain flour
2 teaspoons baking powder
(Makes 12)

1) Line 12 cups of a muffin tray with paper cupcake cases and preheat the oven to 180°C/350°F/Gas Mark 4.

2) Put the cocoa powder in a bowl and whisk in the measured boiling water. Leave to cool.

3) Beat together the butter and sugar until pale and creamy. Gradually beat in the eggs. Sift the flour and baking powder into the bowl and stir well. Once combined, add the cocoa mixture and stir again to mix well.

4) Divide the mixture among the cupcake cases and bake in the oven for about 25 minutes until risen and just firm. Leave in the tin for 10 minutes, then transfer to a wire rack to cool.

Chocolate Chilli Cupcakes

Make *Rich Chocolate Cupcakes*, beating 1 teaspoon of crushed dried chillies with the butter and sugar.

Chocolate Rose Cupcakes

Make *Rich Chocolate Cupcakes*, adding 2 tablespoons of rosewater with the eggs.

Tutti Fruiti Cupcakes

100 ml (3½ fl oz) fruit liqueur (Cointreau, Grand
Marnier, Apricot or Cherry Brandy)
100 g (3½ oz) dried strawberries
100 g (3½ oz) dried blueberries
125 g (4 oz) lightly salted butter, softened
125 g (4 oz) caster sugar
2 eggs
150 g (5 oz) self-raising flour
50 g (2 oz) pistachio nuts, chopped
(Makes 10)

1) Line 10 cups of a muffin tray with paper
cupcake cases and preheat the oven to
180°C/350°F/Gas Mark 4.

2) Put the liqueur in a measuring jug and add
the dried fruits. Use a fork to pierce the fruits.
This will help the liqueur to be absorbed.

3) Put the butter, sugar, eggs and flour in a bowl
and beat with a hand-held electric whisk until
pale and creamy.

4) Drain the unabsorbed liqueur into the bowl
and stir well. Add the fruits and nuts and stir
until evenly combined.

5) Divide the mixture among the cupcake cases
and bake in the oven for about 25 minutes
until risen and just firm. Transfer to a wire
rack to cool.

Exotic Spice Cupcakes

1 lemongrass stalk
100 g (3½ oz) caster sugar
12 cardamom pods
75 g (3 oz) lightly salted butter, softened
2 eggs
50 g (2 oz) fresh root ginger, peeled and finely
grated
200 g (7 oz) plain flour
2 teaspoons baking powder
100 ml (3½ fl oz) milk
100 g (3½ oz) dried mango, chopped
(Makes 10)

1) Line 10 cups of a muffin tray with paper
cupcake cases and preheat the oven to
190°C/375°F/Gas Mark 5.

2) Remove the coarse outer leaves from the
lemongrass, trim off the ends and chop the
core as finely as possible. Whizz in a food

processor with the sugar. Crush the cardamom pods using a pestle and mortar, discard the shells and crush the seeds a little more.

3) Put all the ingredients, except the mango, in a mixing bowl and beat with a hand-held electric whisk until smooth and creamy. Stir in the mango.

4) Divide the mixture among the cupcake cases and bake in the oven for about 20 minutes until risen and just firm. Transfer to a wire rack to cool.

Red Velvet Cupcakes

200 g (7 oz) self-raising flour
2 tablespoons cocoa powder
½ teaspoon bicarbonate of soda
150 ml (¼ pint) buttermilk
1 teaspoon vinegar
1 teaspoon vanilla extract
100 g (3½ oz) lightly salted butter, softened
125 g (4 oz) caster sugar
2 eggs
100 g (3½ oz) raw beetroot, finely grated
(Makes 10)

1) Line 10 cups of a muffin tray with paper cupcake cases and preheat the oven to 180°C/350°F/Gas Mark 4.

2) Combine the flour, cocoa powder and bicarbonate of soda in a bowl. Mix together the buttermilk, vinegar and vanilla in a jug.

3) In a large mixing bowl, beat together the butter and sugar until pale and creamy, then beat in the eggs, grated beetroot and 4 tablespoons of the flour mixture to prevent curdling.

4) Sift half the remaining flour mixture into the bowl and fold in gently with a large metal spoon. Stir in the buttermilk mixture, then sift and fold in the remaining flour until just combined.

5) Divide the mixture among the cupcake cases and bake in the oven for about 25 minutes until risen and just firm. Transfer to a wire rack to cool.

Buttercream

100 g (3½ oz) unsalted butter, softened
150 g (5 oz) icing sugar
(Makes 250 g (8 oz))

1) Put the butter and icing sugar in a bowl and
   beat well with a hand-held electric whisk until
   pale and creamy.

Vodka Buttercream

Make the basic *Buttercream*, then gradually
beat in 5 tablespoons of vodka until the
mixture is smooth.

Amaretto Buttercream

Make the basic *Buttercream*, then gradually
beat in 5 tablespoons of almond liqueur until
the mixture is smooth.

Cream Cheese Frosting

200 g (7 oz) full-fat cream cheese
½ teaspoon vanilla extract
150 g (5 oz) icing sugar
(Makes 350 g (11½ oz))

1) Put all the ingredients in a mixing bowl and
   beat together until smooth and creamy. Chill
   for 1 hour until the frosting has thickened a
   little, then spread or pipe over the cakes.

Coconut Frosting

75 ml (3 fl oz) single cream
50 g (2 oz) coconut cream, chopped if firm
1 tablespoon lime juice
300 g (10 oz) icing sugar
(Makes 400 g (13 oz))

1) Put the single cream and coconut cream in
   a small saucepan and heat gently until the
   coconut has melted. Pour into a mixing bowl

with the lime juice and icing sugar and beat with a hand-held electric whisk until the mixture is thick and smooth. Spread or pipe over the cakes.

Dark Chocolate Ganache
300 ml (½ pint) double cream
300 g (10 oz) plain chocolate, chopped
(Makes 600 g (1 lb 3 oz))

1) Heat the cream in a small saucepan until almost boiling. Pour into a bowl and stir in the chocolate. Leave for a few minutes, stirring frequently, until the chocolate has melted.

2) Leave to cool completely, then chill until the mixture has thickened enough to spread over the cakes. If you are using the ganache for piping, beat it lightly with a hand-held electric whisk to thicken it further.

White Chocolate Ganache
300 ml (½ pint) double cream
300 g (10 oz) white chocolate, chopped
(Makes 600 g (1 lb 3 oz))

1) Heat half the cream in a small saucepan until almost boiling. Pour into a bowl and stir in the chocolate. Leave for a few minutes, stirring frequently, until the chocolate has melted.

2) Leave to cool completely, then stir in the remaining cream and beat with a hand-held electric whisk until the ganache just holds its shape. Don't over-whisk or the texture might spoil.

Decorating Techniques

Using food colourings

Paste food colourings give deep shades. Dot ready-to-roll icing with the paste using the tip of a cocktail stick. Knead the icing on a surface dusted with icing sugar until the colour is evenly distributed. For royal icing, beat small amounts of paste in until you reach the right shade.

Liquid food colourings generally give less intense colours but are good for pastel shades and for painting onto icing.

Powder colourings produce intense shades and can be mixed into icings in the same way as pastes. They are also good for dusting.

Metallic colourings, such as gold and silver, can be bought in liquid form (stir well before use) or as a powder, which can be mixed with a flavourless oil or a dash of vodka so it can be used for painting on. Check colours are edible; if not, remove the decorated area before serving.

As with artists' paints, the best shades are made by mixing basic colours. If you have a limited palette, mix different proportions of red and blue to create lilac, burgundy and purple. Blend red and yellow to make orange. Chestnut brown paste is good for flesh tones, or mix a dash of pink with dark brown.

Making a paper piping bag

Paper piping bags are useful as they're easy to make, disposable after use and don't necessarily require a nozzle for piping fine lines. The amount you snip off the tip will determine the thickness of the line of icing so only snip off a tiny amount at a time. For a more professional finish, fit a fine writing nozzle in the bag.

To make a bag, cut a 25 cm (10 inch) square of greaseproof paper and cut it in half to make two triangles. Place one triangle with the long edge away from you. Curl the right-hand point over and down to meet the lower, centre point. The back of the right-hand point should meet the front of the lower point to form a cone. Now bring the left-hand point over and round the back of the cone so that the three points meet. You may need to slide the points around to get a tightly closed tip. Fold the points over several times to stop the cone unravelling. Snip off a tiny bit of the bag tip, or cut off a bigger piece and insert a piping nozzle, if using. Half-fill the bag with icing and fold over the top.

Making royal icing decorations

Royal icing decorations, such as the kinky boots (see page 92) are made and set on baking parchment. Pipe the shape outlines first using a paper piping bag with a tiny hole in it; make sure there are no gaps in the piping. Then thin the remaining icing with a little water and put it in another piping bag with a slightly larger hole. Use to fill in the shapes, easing the icing into any corners with the tip of a cocktail stick. Leave to harden for about 24 hours before removing the shapes from the paper.

Making icing ruffles

To make icing ruffles, roll out a long strip of ready-to-roll icing on a surface dusted with icing sugar. Roll the end of a cocktail stick along one side of the strip so it becomes ruffled. Lift from the surface and re-dust with icing sugar so the ruffle doesn't stick, then roll with the cocktail stick again. The more you roll the cocktail stick over the icing, the more ruffled the edge will become. Trim the unruffled edge of the strip, to leave a straight edge. Carefully lift the ruffle and position on the cupcake. Once on the cake, ruffles can be lifted and folded with the tip of a cocktail stick.

Melting chocolate

To melt on a hob, chop the chocolate into small pieces and put in a heatproof bowl. Rest the bowl over a pan of very gently simmering water, making sure the base doesn't touch the water. Once the chocolate starts to melt, turn off the heat and leave until completely melted, stirring once or twice. No water or steam from the pan should see into the bowl while the chocolate is melting or it will solidify.

To melt in a microwave, chop the chocolate into small pieces and put in a microwave-proof bowl. Melt in one-minute bursts, checking frequently. Take care, particularly when melting white or milk chocolate, as they have higher sugar contents and are more prone to scorching.

Maneater

275 g (9 oz) plain chocolate, chopped ✳ 1 quantity White Chocolate Ganache (see page 13) ✳ 12 Rich Chocolate Cupcakes (see page 9) ✳ 12 small pink bows (optional) ✳ Makes 12

One: Trace the outline of a female figure onto a piece of baking parchment. It should be roughly 8 cm (3½ inches) from head to toe. For guidance use the photograph opposite, or refer to a book or the Internet to source your image.

Two: Melt the chocolate (see page 15) and put it in a paper piping bag (see page 14). Snip off the merest tip of the bag. Place another sheet of parchment over the female outline. Pipe chocolate around the edges of the shape and then fill in the middle with more chocolate. Slide the top sheet of parchment along so you can pipe more figures. Leave to set.

Three: Spread the ganache over the cooled cupcakes. Carefully peel away the paper from the chocolate shapes and gently push them into the ganache. Decorate the cake cases with pink bows, if liked.

Frill Me!

10 Vanilla Cupcakes (see page 8) ✳ 1 quantity Vodka Buttercream (see page 12) ✳ 325 g (11 oz) black ready~to~roll icing ✳ 250 g (8 oz) white ready~to~roll icing ✳ Icing sugar, for dusting ✳ Makes 10

One: Use a palette knife to spread the cooled cupcakes with the buttercream.

Two: Dust a work surface with icing sugar and roll out 100 g (3½ oz) of the black icing to 5 mm (¼ inch) thick. Cut out 10 hearts using a small cutter. Place on a baking tray lined with baking parchment. Use a thick skewer to impress holes around the edges of the hearts, then leave for several hours to harden.

Three: Roll out a further 25 g (1 oz) of the black icing into a strip about 2 cm (⅞ inch) wide. Ruffle one edge of the strip (see page 15). Lay the ruffled strip around the edges of one cake, pleating it at intervals to give volume and trimming off the excess where the ends join. Use the remaining icing and trimmings and roll more strips to cover the edges of the remaining cakes in the same way.

Four: On a clean surface, use the white icing to create more ruffled strips in the same way and arrange on the cakes, just inside the black ruffles. Repeat, layering the ruffles and finishing with the white. Rest a black heart in the centre of each cake to finish.

Take a Bow

4 egg whites ✹ 200 g (7 oz) icing sugar, plus extra for dusting ✹ ½ teaspoon cream of tartar ✹ Pinch of salt ✹ Deep pink food colouring ✹ 10 Red Velvet Cupcakes (see page 11) ✹ 50 g (2 oz) black ready~to~roll icing ✹ Makes 10

One: Put the egg whites, icing sugar, cream of tartar, salt and a dash of pink food colouring in a heatproof bowl. Rest the bowl over a pan of gently simmering water, making sure the base of the bowl doesn't touch the water. Whisk using a hand-held electric whisk for about 5 minutes until the frosting starts to thicken.

Two: Check the colour of the frosting. If it is too pale, whisk in a little more colouring to make a rich, deep shade of pink. Remove from the heat and whisk for a further 5 minutes or until it forms a softly peaking meringue-like mixture.

Three: Pile the frosting onto the cooled cupcakes and create peaks with a palette knife or the back of a spoon.

Four: Dust a work surface with icing sugar and roll out the black icing thinly. Cut into 1.5 cm x 5 mm (¾ x ¼ inch) rectangles. Pinch the rectangles together in the centres with the tines of two forks to create simple bows. Arrange several bows on each cake.

Hunk o' Love

12 Rich Chocolate Cupcakes (see page 9) ✳ 175 g (6 oz) chocolate hazelnut spread ✳ 500 g (1 lb) flesh~coloured ready~to~roll icing ✳ 100 g (3½ oz) white ready~to~roll icing ✳ Brown food colouring ✳ 50 g (2 oz) burgundy ready~to~roll icing ✳ 15 g (½ oz) black ready~to~roll icing ✳ Icing sugar, for dusting ✳ Makes 12

One: Use a palette knife to spread one half of each cooled cupcake with the chocolate spread.

Two: Dust a work surface with icing sugar. Take a 40 g (1½ oz) piece of flesh-coloured icing and flatten it to about the same diameter as a cake top. Use your fingers to impress chest markings onto the surface. Position on one of the cakes, propping it up on the chocolate spread at the back. Make the remainder in the same way.

Three: Thinly roll out the white icing and cut into thin strips. Position a strip on each side of each chest to resemble an opened shirt. Secure in place with a dampened paintbrush and add buttonholes on one side.

Four: Use a little diluted brown food colouring and a fine paintbrush to paint chest contours and nipples.

Five: Thinly roll out the burgundy icing and cut into long thin strips. Arrange on the cakes to resemble ties. Use the black icing to make three buttons for each cake, make the holes with a cocktail stick and arrange on the shirts.

Dominatrix Delights

100 g (3½ oz) white ready~to~roll icing ✳ 1 quantity Cream Cheese Frosting (see page 12) ✳ Pink food colouring ✳ 10 Vanilla Cupcakes (see page 8) ✳ 100 g (3½ oz) black ready~to~ roll icing ✳ Edible silver food colouring ✳ Icing sugar, for dusting ✳ Makes 10

One: Dust a work surface with icing sugar and thinly roll out the white icing. Cut out 2 small rings for each cake and place on a baking tray lined with baking parchment. This can be done with 2 small cutters, one 1.5 cm (¾ inch) and one 2 cm (⅞ inch) in diameter. Cut out 2 tiny rectangles for each cake to finish the handcuffs and secure to the rings with a dampened paintbrush.

Two: Reroll the trimmings and cut out 10 keys using a small knife. Roll tiny balls of icing and flatten slightly for chains. You'll need 3 for each cake. Leave to harden for at least 2 hours.

Three: Colour the frosting with pink food colouring and use a palette knife to smooth it over the tops of the cooled cupcakes.

Four: Roll out the black icing and cut into very thin strips. Drape over the cakes, letting some loops overhang the edges. To make the tassels, cut out 1.5 x 1 cm (¾ x ½ inch) rectangles. Score through the rectangles, keeping one long edge intact. Dampen the long edge and roll up. Secure to the ends of the black strips by using a dampened paintbrush and pinching them in place.

Five: Use the silver food colouring to paint the handcuffs and keys and allow to dry. Arrange on top of the cakes.

Sealed with a Kiss

100 g (3½ oz) deep red ready~to~roll icing ✹ 200 g (7 oz) white ready~to~roll icing ✹ 10 Red Velvet Cupcakes (see page 11) ✹ ½ quantity Vodka Buttercream (see page 12) ✹ 250 g (8 oz) ivory ready~to~roll icing ✹ Edible gold food colouring ✹ Edible confectioners' glaze ✹ Red food colouring ✹ Icing sugar, for dusting ✹ Makes 10

One: Dust a work surface with icing sugar and roll out the red icing under the palms of your hands to a log shape about 1.5 cm (¾ inch) thick. Cut into 10 lengths, each about 3 cm (1¼ inches) long, making every other cut diagonal to form the points of the lipsticks.

Two: Roll out the white icing to a slightly thicker log and cut into 20 lengths, 10 at 4 cm (1¾ inches) and 10 at 3 cm (1¼ inches) long. Use a dampened paintbrush to secure the red pieces to the longer white pieces. Transfer all the pieces to a baking tray lined with baking parchment and leave to harden overnight.

Three: Use a palette knife to spread the cooled cupcakes with the buttercream, doming it up slightly in the centres. Thinly roll out the ivory icing and cut out 10 discs using an 8 cm (3½ inch) cutter. Arrange over the cupcakes, smoothing down gently.

Four: Use a fine paintbrush to paint the white parts of the lipsticks with gold food colouring. Leave to dry, then paint the red and gold parts with confectioners' glaze.

Five: When dry, secure the lipsticks to the cakes with a dampened paintbrush. Finish by using a fine paintbrush and red food colouring to paint lips to one side of each lipstick.

Hello Sailor!

½ quantity *Dark Chocolate Ganache (see page 13)* ✳ *12 Rich Chocolate Cupcakes (see page 9)* ✳ *250 g (8 oz) flesh~coloured ready~to~roll icing* ✳ *Black and red food colourings* ✳ *Icing sugar, for dusting* ✳ Makes 12

One: Use a palette knife to spread the ganache on the cooled cupcakes.

Two: Dust a work surface with icing sugar, roll out the flesh-coloured icing thinly and cut out 12 discs using an 8 cm (3½ inch) cutter. Place one disc on each cake, smoothing down to eliminate any creases. Leave for several hours or overnight to harden.

Three: Use the food colourings and a fine paintbrush to paint tattoo designs on the icing discs, choosing your own design or copying the one in the photograph.

Dark Angel

400 g (13 oz) black ready~to~roll icing ✳ 25 g (1 oz) red ready~to~roll icing ✳ 200 g (7 oz) royal icing sugar ✳ Black food colouring ✳ 1 quantity Coconut Frosting (see page 12) ✳ 10 Vanilla Cupcakes (see page 8) ✳ Icing sugar, for dusting ✳ 3.6 m (12 ft) ribbon ✳ Makes 10

One: Divide the black icing into 10 equal pieces and cut each piece in half. Dust your hands with icing sugar and mould each piece into a wing, 10 left and 10 right, each about 4 cm (1¾ inches) deep and 6 cm (2½ inches) wide. Press 2 wings together to form a pair, securing with a dampened paintbrush. Place on a baking tray lined with baking parchment.

Two: Dust a work surface with icing sugar and roll out the red icing. Cut out tiny hearts using a 1 cm (½ inch) cutter. Transfer to the baking tray.

Three: Put the royal icing sugar in a bowl and add enough water, about 5 teaspoons, to mix to a smooth paste. Beat in the black food colouring. Put the icing in a paper piping bag (see page 14) and snip off the merest tip. Use to pipe a lacy design all over the wings. Position a red heart in the centre of each. Leave for several hours or overnight to harden.

Four: Use a palette knife to spread the frosting over the tops of the cooled cupcakes. Carefully position a set of wings on each cake.

Five: Cut a 30 cm (12 inch) length of ribbon and tie around each cupcake case to decorate. You might need to apply a dot of glue around the back to hold the ribbon in place.

Temptation

325 g (11 oz) white almond paste ❋ Purple and dark green food colourings ❋ 150 g (5 oz) pale green ready~to~roll icing ❋ 1 quantity Amaretto Buttercream (see page 12) ❋ 10 Cherry Cupcakes (see page 8) ❋ Icing sugar, for dusting ❋ Makes 10

One: Divide the almond paste into 10 equal pieces. Dust your hands with icing sugar, roll each piece into a ball and pinch out a point on one side. Cut off the tip of the point. Paint the tips of the figs green and the rest purple. For the most effective results, refer to a photograph of a fig to get the colours just right.

Two: Dust a work surface with icing sugar and roll out the green icing as thinly as possible. Cut out fig leaves using cutters in two or three sizes. If you can't get fig leaf cutters, use an ivy cutter. Mark veins on the leaves with the tip of a knife. Twist into natural shapes and transfer to a sheet of crumpled foil. Leave for several hours or overnight to harden.

Three: Once the leaves are hard, paint them with dark green food colouring.

Four: Use a palette knife to spread the buttercream over the cooled cupcakes and gently press the figs on top. Arrange the leaves around the figs, resting them on the buttercream and securing onto the figs with dots of buttercream.

Devilishly Good

1 quantity *Dark Chocolate Ganache (see page 13)* ✸ 12 *Chocolate Chilli Cupcakes (see page 9)* ✸ 24 *small fresh red chillies* ✸ *Edible red dusting powder* ✸ 2.6 m (8¼ ft) *feather boa* ✸ Makes 12

One: Put the chocolate ganache in a large paper piping bag (see page 14) fitted with a large star nozzle. Pipe a lavish swirl of ganache on top of each cooled cupcake and position 2 small red chillies on top.

Two: Use your fingers to sprinkle a little red dusting powder over each cake. Cut 12 lengths out of the feather boa, then wrap a length round each cake case, holding it in place with a little blob of glue.

Thorny Passion

1 quantity Coconut Frosting (see page 12) ✻ *10 Red Velvet Cupcakes (see page 11)*
✻ *650 g (1 lb 6 oz) deep red ready~to~roll icing* ✻ *Clear piping gel (optional)* ✻ *Icing sugar,*
for dusting ✻ Makes 10

One: Use a palette knife to spread the frosting over the cupcakes. Divide the red icing into 10 equal pieces.

Two: Take one piece of icing and wrap the other pieces tightly in cling film. Dust your hands with icing sugar, break off a grape-sized piece and shape it into a cone, pressing the thick end down on a work surface. Pinch the cone in near the base to form a 'waist'.

Three: Take a small ball of icing and shape it into a petal, pressing it as thin as possible until it is about 3 cm (1¼ inches) in diameter. The finer the petals are, the more realistic the rose will be. Wrap the petal around the cone so it curls tightly around the top to form the centre of the rose.

Four: Shape another slightly larger petal and wrap around the cone on the opposite side. Continue layering the petals, making each slightly larger than the one before and opening them out as you work away from the centre. Roll the top edges of the outer petals for a realistic effect.

Five: Slice the rose off the work surface and transfer to one of the cakes, then make the remainder in the same way. Put a spoonful of piping gel in a paper piping bag (see page 14) and snip off the tip. Pipe drops of gel onto the rose petals, if liked.

Frills and Thrills

250 g (8 oz) flesh~coloured ready~to~roll icing ✳ 100 g (3½ oz) black ready~to~roll icing ✳ 1 quantity White Chocolate Ganache (see page 13) ✳ Turquoise food colouring ✳ 10 Tutti Fruiti Cupcakes (see page 10) ✳ 3 m (10 ft) black beading ✳ Icing sugar, for dusting ✳ Makes 10

One: Divide the flesh-coloured icing into 10 equal pieces, dust your hands with icing sugar and shape each piece into a bottom with thighs and waist. Place the bottoms on a baking tray lined with baking parchment.

Two: Dust a work surface with icing sugar, roll out the black icing thinly and cut out 10 skimpy knickers. Secure onto the bottoms using a dampened paintbrush.

Three: Reroll the black icing trimmings and cut a strip about 5 mm (¼ inch) wide. Ruffle one edge of the strip (see page 15). Trim off the unfrilled edge and secure the frill to the knickers, cutting off the excess at the sides. Repeat to make 2 frills on each pair of knickers.

Four: Colour the ganache with turquoise food colouring, then spread over the tops of the cooled cupcakes with a palette knife. Position the decorations on top and tie strings of beads around the sides of the cake cases, securing with a little glue at the back if necessary.

Wandering Hands

350 g (11½ oz) black ready~to~roll icing ✳ Edible confectioners' glaze ✳ 100 g (3½ oz) lilac ready~to~roll icing ✳ 10 Exotic Spice Cupcakes (see page 10) ✳ 1 quantity Cream Cheese Frosting (see page 12) ✳ Icing sugar, for dusting ✳ Makes 10

One: Take a 25 g (1 oz) piece of black icing and cut in half. Dust your hands with icing sugar, then shape each piece into a hand, 10 left and 10 right. The easiest way is to make a roll about 5 cm (2 inches) long with a mitten shape at the end. Make 4 cuts with the tip of a knife to shape fingers and thumb, then roll the fingers slightly to smooth out the cut edges. Place the hands in pairs on a baking tray lined with baking parchment, then bend them back at the wrists. Paint the hands with edible confectioners' glaze and leave them to dry.

Two: Cut the lilac icing into 10 equal pieces, then shape each into a perfume bottle with a lid. Sit the bottles in the palms of the hands. Push a wooden cocktail stick up through the base of each hand and into the bottle, leaving a little of the stick protruding at each wrist. Leave to harden for several hours or overnight.

Three: Spread the cooled cupcakes with the frosting. Carefully lift the hands from the paper and press the sticks down gently into the cakes.

Four: Use the remaining black icing to make the roses. Take a pea-sized piece of black icing and roll it under your fingers until about 5 cm (2 inches) long. Press flat so until it about 5 mm (¼ inch) wide, then roll up to resemble a simple rose shape. Press gently into the icing around the top edges of the cakes.

Burlesque Bites

1 vanilla pod ✳ 1 quantity Vodka Buttercream (see page 12) ✳ 10 Vanilla Cupcakes (see page 8) ✳ 150 g (5 oz) black ready~to~roll icing ✳ Black writing icing ✳ Edible gold food colouring ✳ 3 m (10 ft) fine ribbon ✳ Icing sugar, for dusting ✳ Makes 10

One: Split the vanilla pod lengthways with the tip of a sharp knife. Scrape out the seeds and mix in a bowl with a tablespoon of the buttercream to distribute the seeds evenly. Beat in the remaining buttercream and spread over the cooled cupcakes with a palette knife.

Two: Dust your hands with icing sugar. Take 10 g (⅓ oz) of black icing and mould it into the shape of a basque. Dust a work surface with icing sugar, then thinly roll out a little more of the black icing into a strip about 5 mm (¼ inch) wide. Ruffle one edge of the strip (see page 15). Dampen the unfrilled edge with a paintbrush. Secure a frill to both top and bottom edges of the basque, trimming off any excess.

Three: Position the basque on one of the cakes, then make the remainder in the same way. Pipe a row of buttons down the centre of each basque using the black writing icing. Paint the buttons with gold food colouring.

Four: Cut a 30 cm (12 inch) length of ribbon and tie around each cupcake case to decorate. You might need to apply a dot of glue around the back to hold the ribbon in place.

Je t'aime

100 g (3½ oz) each of white, lilac and pink ready~to~roll icing ✳ White writing icing ✳ Red and black food colourings ✳ 10 Vanilla Cupcakes (see page 8) ✳ 1 quantity White Chocolate Ganache (see page 13) ✳ Icing sugar, for dusting ✳ Makes 10

One: Dust a work surface with icing sugar and roll out the white icing to 2.5 mm (⅛ inch) thick. Cut out discs using a 3 cm (1¼ inch) cutter. Transfer to a baking tray lined with baking parchment and reroll the trimmings to make more discs. Repeat with the lilac and pink icings. Leave to harden for at least 2 hours or overnight.

Two: Use the white writing icing to pipe a heart onto each disc. Use red and black food colourings and a fine paintbrush to decorate the discs with little hearts or messages and leave to dry.

Three: Use a palette knife to spread the cupcakes with the chocolate ganache. Arrange the icing discs on the cooled cupcakes, securing in place with the writing icing left in the tube.

Heaven Scent

1 quantity White Chocolate Ganache (see page 13) ✸ 12 Chocolate Rose Cupcakes (see page 9)
✸ 125 g (4 oz) black ready~to~roll icing ✸ 125 g (4 oz) white ready~to~roll icing ✸ 125 g (4 oz)
ivory ready~to~roll icing ✸ Edible pearlized pink dusting powder ✸ Edible silver food colouring
✸ Large silver balls ✸ Icing sugar, for dusting ✸ Makes 12

One: Place the ganache in a paper piping bag (see page 14) fitted with a star nozzle and pipe over the tops of the cooled cupcakes.

Two: Reserve 15 g (½ oz) of the black icing. Dust a work surface with icing sugar and roll the remaining black icing into a rope about 50 cm (20 inches) long. Roll the white icing to the same length, then roll it slightly with the black rope until the two hold together. Fold the rope in half and roll again into a 50 cm (20 inch) rope. Repeat two or three times until the icing is streaked black and white. Finally, roll the icing into a 60 cm (24 inch) rope and cut into 12 equal pieces.

Three: Flatten each piece slightly and shape into a female form, narrowing in the centre, pinching out breasts and extending the shoulders slightly. Push one gently onto each cake. Shape the reserved black icing into little stoppers and secure them with a dampened paintbrush.

Four: Thinly roll out the ivory icing and cut into 1 cm (½ inch) strips. Dust both sides with pink dusting powder. Drape them, ribbon like, around the cakes and leave to harden.

Five: Use a fine paintbrush to paint the tops of the stoppers with silver food colouring. Tuck several silver balls in place, pushing them gently into the ganache.

Fallen Angel

10 Vanilla Cupcakes (see page 8) ✻ 1 quantity Coconut Frosting (see page 12)
✻ 4 tablespoons caster sugar ✻ Edible red glitter ✻ 10 birthday cake candles ✻ Vegetable oil,
for brushing ✻ Makes 10

One: Use a palette knife to spread the cooled cupcakes with coconut frosting.

Two: Line a large baking tray with a double thickness of kitchen paper, then completely cover the baking tray with foil. Press a 5–6 cm (2–2½ inch) heart-shaped cutter onto the foil. The paper underneath the foil will help create an impression of the shape. Press 11 more hearts onto the foil. Brush the hearts lightly with vegetable oil.

Three: Sprinkle about a teaspoon of sugar into each heart shape, defining the edges well but thinning out the sugar in the centre of each heart. Place the baking tray under a preheated hot grill and cook, watching closely, for a few minutes until most of the sugar has melted to a very pale caramel but some sugar crystals remain. Leave to cool.

Four: Carefully peel away the foil from the hearts, then sprinkle a fine trail of glitter around the edges of each. Press the hearts down gently into the frosting and sprinkle a little more dusting powder on the cakes. Position a candle behind each heart, ready for lighting.

Blond Ambition

10 Tutti Fruiti cupcakes (see page 10) ✴ 7 tablespoons strawberry jam ✴ 4 egg whites
✴ Pink food colouring ✴ 200 g (7 oz) caster sugar ✴ Silver balls ✴ Edible silver leaf
✴ Makes 10

One: Use a teaspoon to scoop out a small cavity from the centre of each cupcake and spoon in the jam. Preheat the oven to 220°C/425°F/Gas Mark 7.

Two: Whisk the egg whites with plenty of food colouring until softly peaking. Gradually add the sugar, a tablespoonful at a time, whisking between each addition until the meringue is thick and glossy. Put half the meringue in a large paper piping bag (see page 14) fitted with a 1 cm (½ inch) plain nozzle and pipe deep swirls of meringue onto half the cakes, finishing with a point on top of each. Keep the meringue inside the paper cases as it will expand slightly during baking. Repeat with the remainder.

Three: Gently press the silver balls into the meringue. Bake in the preheated oven for 8–10 minutes until the meringue is just beginning to colour. Leave to cool.

Four: Decorate the meringue with silver leaf. Tear off small pieces of leaf with tweezers and lay them on the meringue, then gently flatten out with a soft paintbrush.

Forbidden Fruits

300 g (10 oz) red ready~to~roll icing ✳ 10 cloves ✳ Red and brown food colourings ✳ Edible confectioners' glaze ✳ 10 Tutti Fruiti Cupcakes (see page 10) ✳ 1 quantity Cream Cheese Frosting (see page 12) ✳ 150 g (5 oz) dark orange ready~to~roll icing ✳ Icing sugar, for dusting ✳ Makes 10

One: Divide the red icing into 10 equal pieces, dust a work surface with icing sugar and roll each piece into a ball. Flatten the tops slightly and push a clove into each to resemble an apple stalk. Use the food colourings to paint darker areas on the apples, place on a baking tray lined with baking parchment and brush with the confectioners' glaze. Allow to dry.

Two: Use a palette knife to spread the cooled cupcakes with the cream cheese frosting. Position an apple on top of each cake.

Three: Divide the orange icing into 10 equal pieces and roll each under the palm of your hand to shape a snake. Make one end thicker than the other, flattening it slightly into a head and tapering the thin end to a point. Each snake should be about 23 cm (9 inches) long.

Four: Coil the snakes around the apples, letting the tails hang over the sides of the cake cases. Use the food colourings and a fine paintbrush to paint the details on the snakes.

Dressed to Kill

250 g (8 oz) red ready-to-roll icing ✳ 250 g (8 oz) brandy-flavoured almond paste
✳ 10 Cherry Cupcakes (see page 8) ✳ 250 g (8 oz) icing sugar, plus extra for dusting
✳ Black food colouring ✳ Makes 10

One: Take 20 g (¾ oz) of red icing and divide equally in half. Dust your hands with icing sugar and mould the pieces of icing into a pair of shoes, either copying the photograph opposite or using a design of your choice. Transfer to a baking tray lined with baking parchment and leave to harden while shaping the remainder.

Two: Cut the almond paste into 10 even-sized pieces and flatten into small, slightly domed discs, about 5 cm (2 inches) in diameter. Position a disc on the centre of each cooled cupcake.

Three: Put the icing sugar in a small bowl and stir in enough water, about 6–7 teaspoons, to make a smooth paste that thickly coats the back of the spoon. Spread over the cakes to cover the almond paste and run almost to the edges of the cakes.

Four: Position a pair of shoes on each cake, then use a fine paintbrush to decorate the shoes with black food colouring.

Girl's Best Friend

6 clear mints ✸ 125 g (4 oz) ivory ready~to~roll icing ✸ 10 Red Velvet Cupcakes (see page 11) ✸ ½ quantity Cream Cheese Frosting (see page 12) ✸ 300 g (10 oz) pink ready~to~roll icing ✸ 125 g (4 oz) blue ready~to~roll icing ✸ Edible pearlized dusting powder ✸ Fine floristry wire ✸ Edible silver food colouring ✸ Icing sugar, for dusting ✸ Makes 10

One: Put the mints in a polythene bag and lightly crush with a rolling pin. Dust a work surface with icing sugar and roll out the ivory icing. Cut out 10 rectangles, each 3.5 x 2.5 cm (1½ x 1 inch). Brush with a dampened paintbrush and press pieces of mint into the icing.

Two: Cut out 10 strips, each 6 x 1 cm (2½ x ½ inch), and bend the ends into a ring. Transfer all the pieces to a baking tray lined with baking parchment and leave to harden for at least 2 hours. Wrap the trimmings in cling film and set aside.

Three: Use a palette knife to spread the cooled cupcakes with the frosting. Thinly roll out the pink icing and cut out 10 discs using an 8 cm (3½ inch) cutter. Place one on top of each cake.

Four: Shape tiny balls from the remaining ivory icing and the blue icing, rolling the ivory balls in pearl dusting powder. Thread rows of balls onto 8 cm (3½ inch) lengths of floristry wire and drape around the cakes, pushing the wire ends into the icing to hold in place. Use a dampened paintbrush to secure more balls on the icing.

Five: Paint the rings using silver food colouring, allow to dry and secure on the tops of the cakes.

Luscious Lips

1 quantity Buttercream (see page 12) ✻ 10 Tutti Fruiti Cupcakes (see page 10)
✻ 150 g (5 oz) red ready~to~roll icing ✻ 1 tablespoon strawberry jam ✻ Icing sugar, for dusting
✻ Makes 10

One: Spread the buttercream over the tops of the cooled cupcakes using a palette knife.

Two: Take 15 g (½ oz) of the red icing, dust your hands with icing sugar and mould the icing into the shape of a pair of lips. Position on one of the cakes, then shape the remainder in the same way.

Three: Pass the strawberry jam through a sieve to remove any lumps. Use a small paintbrush to brush the jam over the lips to give a glossy sheen.

Feel the Heat

250 g (8 oz) chilli~flavoured plain chocolate, chopped ✱ 15 g (½ oz) unsalted butter ✱ 12 Chocolate Chilli Cupcakes (see page 9) ✱ 400 g (13 oz) red ready~to~roll icing ✱ 50 g (2 oz) white ready~to~roll icing ✱ Black food colouring ✱ Icing sugar, for dusting ✱ Makes 12

One: Melt the chocolate with the butter (see page 15). Once the chocolate has cooled and thickened slightly, but not set, spoon a little over the top of each cooled cupcake and use a palette knife to smooth.

Two: Roll 20 g (¾ oz) of red icing into a ball and flatten until it is about 5 cm (2 inches) in diameter. Dust your fingers with icing sugar and shape small pieces of white icing to make a mouth and eyes. Position on the red icing disc, securing with a dampened paintbrush.

Three: Roll very thin ropes of red icing and position around the mouth and tops of the eyes. Shape and position horns and a nose. Position the face on one of the cakes, then use a little more red icing to make a pointy tail to drape round the sides of the cake. Repeat with the remaining cakes.

Four: Use the black food colouring and a fine paintbrush to finish the eyes and mouth.

Caged

10 Tutti Fruiti Cupcakes (see page 10) ✳ 1 quantity White Chocolate Ganache (see page 13) ✳ 5 oranges ✳ 100 g (3½ oz) clear mints ✳ 4 tablespoons strawberry conserve ✳ 10 fresh strawberries ✳ Vegetable oil, for brushing ✳ Makes 10

One: Preheat the oven to 200°C/400°F/Gas Mark 6. Use a palette knife to swirl the cooled cupcakes with the ganache. Brush the oranges with vegetable oil, wrap them tightly in cling film and place on a work surface with the cling film ends underneath. Brush again lightly with vegetable oil.

Two: Make a small bowl out of a piece of foil, place on a baking tray and unwrap half the mints into it. Put in the preheated oven for about 15 minutes or until the mints have melted and the syrup is bubbling.

Three: Working quickly, dip a fork into the mint syrup and drizzle it back and forth across the top half of an orange. Repeat the dipping and drizzling, crisscrossing until the orange is fairly thickly coated in fine lines of syrup. Repeat on the remaining oranges. If the syrup hardens before you've had time to coat all the oranges, return it to the oven to soften again.

Four: Leave the syrup until brittle, then carefully unravel the cling film and pull out the oranges. Ease the film away from the cages and transfer them to a lightly oiled sheet of foil. Make 5 more cages in the same way with the remaining mints.

Five: Press the strawberry conserve through a sieve to remove any lumps. Position a cage at a tilted angle on each cake and perch a strawberry inside. Drizzle with the conserve.

Luscious in Leather

12 Rich Chocolate Cupcakes (see page 9) ✳ 1 quantity Dark Chocolate Ganache (see page 13) ✳ 75 g (3 oz) each of black, lilac and deep pink ready~to~roll icing ✳ Black writing icing ✳ Silver balls ✳ Icing sugar, for dusting ✳ Makes 12

One: Use a palette knife to spread the cooled cupcakes with the ganache, doming it up in the centre and spreading it down as smoothly as possible.

Two: Dust a work surface with icing sugar, thinly roll out the black icing and cut into thin strips. Arrange one piece on each cake to make a belt, trimming off the ends to fit. Make holes in the remaining black strips and lay on top of the belts at one end, securing them in place with a dampened paintbrush. Make more belts with the lilac and pink icings.

Three: Use the writing icing to pipe buckles on some of the belts and the silver balls to make buckles on the others, holding them in place with tiny blobs of writing icing.

Drive Me Wild

12 Chocolate Chilli Cupcakes (see page 9) ✳ ½ quantity Vodka Buttercream (see page 12) ✳ 250 g (8 oz) white ready~to~roll icing ✳ Orange and brown food colourings ✳ 50 g (2 oz) black ready~to~roll icing ✳ 75 g (3 oz) red ready~to~roll icing ✳ Pink or red dusting powder (optional) ✳ Icing sugar, for dusting ✳ Makes 12

One: Use a small palette knife to spread the cooled cakes with the buttercream, doming it up in the centres.

Two: Colour the white icing with orange food colouring (see page 14), adding a dash of brown if the orange is very bright. Now separate 50 g (2 oz) of the orange icing and work in some brown colouring to darken it. Wrap the two colours separately in cling film and set aside.

Three: Dust a work surface with icing sugar and roll out 15 g (½ oz) of the orange icing to form a 6 cm (2½ inch) disc. Break off tiny balls of the black icing, flatten them slightly and press gently onto the orange disc, spacing them about 5 mm (¼ inch) apart. Press even smaller balls of brown icing on top of the black icing. Using a rolling pin, gently roll the icing so the colours merge. Cut out a disc using an 8 cm (3½ inch) cutter and position over one of the cakes, tucking the icing in around the edges. Repeat with the remaining cakes.

Four: Shape the red icing into little handbags, add a black clasp to each and secure on the tops of the cakes with a dampened paintbrush. Finish by dusting the handbags with the dusting powder, if liked.

Peek~a~boo!

10 Red Velvet Cupcakes (see page 11) ✻ ½ quantity Vodka Buttercream (see page 12) ✻ 400 g (13 oz) flesh~coloured ready~to~roll icing ✻ 250 g (8 oz) royal icing sugar ✻ Dark blue and edible gold food colourings ✻ Piping sparkles (optional) ✻ Icing sugar, for dusting ✻ Makes 10

One: Use a palette knife to spread the cooled cupcakes with the buttercream.

Two: Dust your hands with icing sugar, take a 20 g (¾ oz) ball of flesh-coloured icing and cut in half. Flatten each half slightly into a breast shape and position on one of the cakes. Repeat with the remainder.

Three: Dust a work surface with icing sugar and thinly roll out the remaining icing. Cut out 10 discs using an 8 cm (3½ inch) cutter. Lay them over the cakes, smoothing to fit and eliminating any creases.

Four: Beat the royal icing sugar in a bowl with 5–6 teaspoons of water to make a smooth icing that only just holds its shape. Set aside one-third of the icing in a separate bowl and colour the remainder dark blue. Spoon the blue icing into a paper piping bag (see page 10) fitted with a writer nozzle and use to pipe lacy bra designs onto the breasts.

Five: Put the reserved white icing in another piping bag fitted with a writer nozzle and pipe little flowers and a necklace. Leave the icing to set before painting the necklaces and flowers with gold food colouring. Pipe a dot of piping sparkles in the middle of each necklace, if liked.

Strangers in the Night

200 g (7 oz) royal icing sugar ✳ Deep red food colouring ✳ 10 Red Velvet Cupcakes (see page 11) ✳ 1 quantity Vodka Buttercream (see page 12) ✳ 250 g (8 oz) orange ready~to~roll icing ✳ 50 g (2 oz) black ready~to~roll icing ✳ Black writing icing ✳ Icing sugar, for dusting ✳ Makes 10

One: Trace the outline of a mask onto a piece of baking parchment. It should be roughly 8 cm (3½ inches) across. For guidance use the photograph opposite, or refer to a book or the Internet to source your image.

Two: Put the royal icing sugar in a bowl and add enough water, about 5 teaspoons, to mix to a smooth paste. Beat in the red food colouring. Put a third of the icing in a paper piping bag (see page 14) and snip off the merest tip.

Three: Place another sheet of parchment over the outline. Pipe icing around the shape, then pipe another wavy edge round the outside. Slide the top sheet of parchment along so you can pipe more masks. Add a few drops of water to the remaining icing, put in another piping bag with a larger hole and fill in the centres of the masks. Leave to harden overnight.

Four: Spread the cooled cupcakes with buttercream. Dust a work surface with icing sugar, roll out the orange icing and cut 10 discs using an 8 cm (3½ inch) cutter. Position a disc on each cake, then secure the masks in place with a dampened paintbrush. Roll out the black icing and cut into strips, then attach one to each cake. Finish by using the black writing icing to pipe a border round each mask.

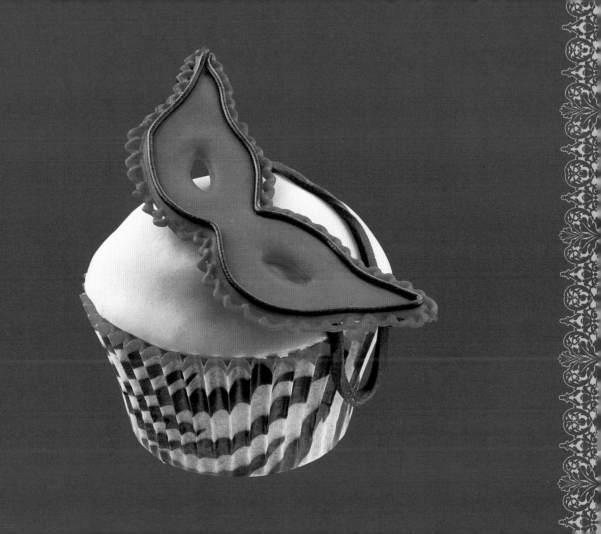

Sex Kitten

1 quantity Vodka Buttercream (see page 12) ✻ 10 Vanilla Cupcakes (see page 8)
✻ 250 g (8 oz) white ready~to~roll icing ✻ Pink and black food colourings ✻ 125 g (4 oz) black
ready~to~roll icing ✻ 50 g (2 oz) deep pink ready~to~roll icing ✻ Edible gold food colouring
✻ Icing sugar, for dusting ✻ Makes 10

One: Use a palette knife to spread the buttercream over the tops of the cooled cupcakes.

Two: Dust a work surface with icing sugar, roll out the white icing thinly and cut out 10 discs using an 8 cm (3½ inch) cutter. Position a disc on each cake and smooth gently. Gather up the trimmings and knead in a little pink food colouring to make a pale pink icing. Wrap in cling film and set aside.

Three: Thinly roll out the black icing and cut out an 8 cm (3½ inch) disc. Press the cutter into the disc to create a crescent and secure on one of the cakes using a dampened paintbrush. Repeat with the remaining cakes, rerolling the trimmings to make more crescents. Use more of the black icing to make ears and position on the cakes. Reserve the trimmings.

Four: Thinly roll out the deep pink ready-to-roll icing and use the cutter and a knife to shape the hair. Use the trimmings to shape lips.

Five: Use the pale pink icing to make the centres of the ears, the noses and collars. Use a fine paintbrush and black food colouring to paint eyes and whiskers. Thinly roll the reserved black icing and cut out long curvy eyelashes. Secure in place and finish by painting gold spots on the collars.

Love Bites

10 Red Velvet Cupcakes (see page 11) ✳ ½ quantity Cream Cheese Frosting (see page 12)
✳ 250 g (8 oz) burgundy ready~to~roll icing ✳ 300 g (10 oz) black ready~to~roll icing
✳ 125 g (4 oz) white ready~to~roll icing ✳ Brown writing icing ✳ Black food colouring
✳ 25 g (1 oz) red ready~to roll icing ✳ Icing sugar, for dusting ✳ Makes 10

One: Use a palette knife to spread the cream cheese frosting on the cooled cupcakes. Dust a work surface with icing sugar, thinly roll out the burgundy icing and cut out 10 discs using an 8 cm (3½ inch) cutter. Position on the cakes. Reserve the trimmings.

Two: Reserve 25 g (1 oz) of black icing for the collars and divide the remainder into 10 pieces. Roll out one piece into a 20 cm (8 inch) strip, 4 cm (1¾ inches) wide at one end tapering to 2 cm (⅞ inch) at the other. Dampen the edge of a cake with a paintbrush and wrap the strip around it, tucking the narrower end behind the wide end. Repeat with the remainder. Thinly roll out the black icing trimmings, cut out 10 bats and add balls of burgundy icing for eyes.

Three: Work a small piece of burgundy icing into the white icing to make it pink. Roll into balls for heads and press into position, then make 10 hands and secure behind the cloaks. Thinly roll out the reserved black and burgundy icings, place one on top of the other and reroll. Cut into 3 cm (1¼ inch) wide strips and then into rectangles with one side longer than the other. Secure behind the heads for collars.

Four: Scribble brown writing icing onto the heads for hair and use a fine paintbrush and black food colouring to paint features on the faces. Shape tiny pieces of red icing into drips of blood and use a dampened paintbrush to secure them to the cloaks. Gently press the bats onto the sides of the cakes. If they don't stick, use a little of the frosting to secure them.

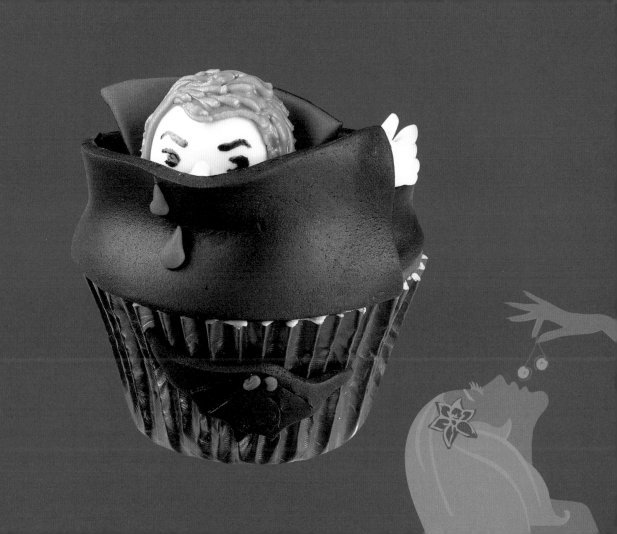

Cupid's Revenge

200 g (7 oz) deep red ready~to~roll icing ✳ 400 g (13 oz) icing sugar, plus extra for dusting ✳ 3~4 tablespoons lemon juice ✳ Black food colouring ✳ 10 Red Velvet Cupcakes (see page 11) ✳ Makes 10

One: Dust a work surface with icing sugar and thickly roll out the red icing. Cut out 10 hearts using a 3.5 cm (1½ inch) cutter. Use the tip of a sharp knife to cut off about one-third of each heart in a jagged line. Push a piece of wooden cocktail stick up through the base of each piece. Transfer all the pieces to a baking tray lined with baking parchment and leave for at least 2 hours to harden. Wrap the icing trimmings in cling film and set aside.

Two: Beat the icing sugar in a bowl with enough lemon juice to make an icing that thickly covers the back of a spoon. Transfer one-third of the icing to a separate bowl and colour it dark grey using black food colouring.

Three: Spread the white icing over the cooled cupcakes, allowing it to drizzle down the sides. If it is too thick to drizzle, add a drop more lemon juice. If it is too runny, beat in a little more icing sugar. Drizzle the grey icing over the white.

Four: While the icing is still wet, shape the red icing trimmings into small teardrops and push gently into the icing at the front and down the sides of the cakes. Secure the heart pieces to the cakes by pushing the cocktail sticks down into the cakes.

Baby Doll

12 Rich Chocolate Cupcakes (see page 9) ✳ ½ quantity Dark Chocolate Ganache (see page 13)
✳ 500 g (1 lb) white almond paste ✳ Pink food colouring ✳ 250 g (8 oz) royal icing sugar
✳ 75 g (3 oz) black ready~to~roll icing ✳ Icing sugar, for dusting ✳ Makes 12

One: Use a palette knife to spread the cupcakes with the ganache. Take a piece of almond paste the size of a walnut and cut in half. Shape into two balls, flatten slightly and press into the ganache 1 cm (½ inch) apart near one edge of a cake. Repeat with the other cakes.

Two: Dust a work surface with icing sugar and knead a little pink food colouring into the remaining paste. Roll out thinly and cut out 12 discs using an 8 cm (3½ inch) cutter. Cut off a 1 cm (½ inch) strip from the two opposite sides of the discs to give straight sides and lay over the cakes, smoothing around the breasts. Use a fine paintbrush and a little food colouring to paint nipples.

Three: Put the royal icing sugar in a bowl and add enough water, about 6–7 teaspoons, to mix to a smooth paste. Put two-thirds in a paper piping bag (see page 14) fitted with a fine writer nozzle. Use to pipe lacy baby doll nighties over the cakes.

Four: Roll out the black icing thinly, cut into 1 cm (½ inch) wide strips and ruffle the strips (see page 15). Position on the nighties so the ruffles overhang the edges of the cakes. Colour the remaining piping icing pink and put in another piping bag. Use to pipe the decorative trim.

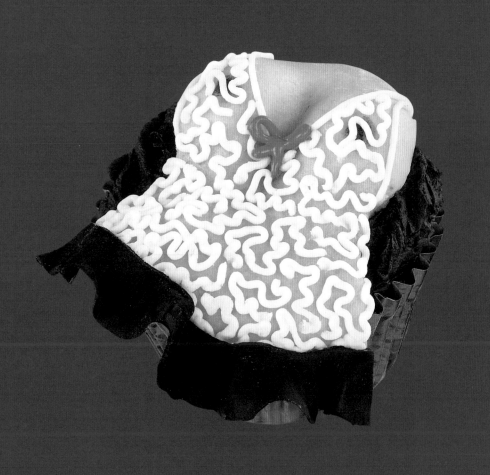

Love Birds

200 g (7 oz) royal icing sugar ✳ Ivory and navy blue food colourings ✳ 10 Exotic Spice Cupcakes (see page 10) ✳ ½ quantity Buttercream (see page 12) ✳ 300 g (10 oz) icing sugar ✳ Makes 10

One: Trace the outlines of 2 love birds onto a piece of baking parchment. They should be roughly 5 cm (2 inches) from beak to tail. For guidance use the photograph opposite, or refer to a book or the Internet to source your image.

Two: Put the royal icing sugar in a bowl and add enough water, about 5–6 teaspoons, to mix to a smooth paste. Beat in a few drops of ivory food colouring.

Three: Put a third of the icing in a paper piping bag (see page 14) and snip off the merest tip. Place another sheet of parchment over the bird outlines. Pipe icing around the edges of the shapes, then slide the top sheet of parchment along so you can pipe more birds. Use the remaining icing in the bag to pipe some hearts.

Four: Add a few drops of water to the remaining icing, put in another piping bag with a larger hole and fill in the centres of the birds and hearts. Leave to harden overnight.

Five: Use a palette knife to spread the cooled cupcakes with the buttercream. Put the icing sugar in a bowl and add about 2–3 tablespoons water, enough to make a smooth icing that coats the back of the spoon. Beat in navy blue food colouring and spread over the cakes. Position the birds and hearts on the cakes, securing the hearts with icing and propping the birds with cocktail sticks if necessary.

Eastern Promise

300 g (10 oz) plain chocolate, chopped ✱ 12 Chocolate Rose Cupcakes (see page 9) ✱ 500 g (1 lb) rose~flavoured Turkish delight, chopped ✱ Silver balls ✱ Makes 12

One: Melt the chocolate (see page 15) and spread a teaspoonful over the top of each cooled cupcake.

Two: Pile lots of chopped Turkish delight on top of each cake.

Three: Use a teaspoon to drizzle chocolate over the tops of the cakes so it falls over and between the Turkish delight, without completely coating it. Finish the cakes with silver balls. These cakes are best served on the day they're decorated.

French Fancy

250 g (8 oz) royal icing sugar ❋ Black food colouring ❋ 10 Tutti Fruiti Cupcakes (see page 10) ❋ ½ quantity Buttercream (see page 12) ❋ 125 g (4 oz) each of dark blue, turquoise and deep pink ready~to~roll icing ❋ Icing sugar, for dusting ❋ Makes 10

One: Trace the outline of a pair of kicking legs, roughly 8 cm (3½ inches) long, onto a piece of baking parchment. For guidance use the picture opposite, or refer to a book or the Internet to source your image.

Two: Put the royal icing sugar in a bowl and add enough water, about 6 teaspoons, to mix to a smooth paste. Beat in the black food colouring. Put a third of the icing in a paper piping bag (see page 14) and snip off the merest tip.

Three: Place another sheet of parchment over the outline. Pipe icing around the shape, then slide the top sheet of parchment along so you can pipe more legs. Add a few drops of water to the remaining icing, put in another piping bag with a larger hole and fill in the centres of the shapes. Leave to harden overnight.

Four: Use a palette knife to spread the cooled cupcakes with the buttercream. Dust a work surface with icing sugar and roll out some of the blue ready-to-roll icing into a strip about 2 cm (¾ inch) wide. Ruffle one edge of the strip (see page 15). Lay the ruffled strips around the edges of the cakes.

Five: Use the pink and turquoise icings to shape more ruffles and arrange on the cakes. Use turquoise icing to make garters, securing with a dampened paintbrush. Make a slit in the centre of each cake with a knife and press the legs into position.

Cheek to Cheek

10 *Tutti Fruiti Cupcakes (see page 10)* ❋ *½ quantity Buttercream (see page 12)*
❋ *500 g (1 lb) flesh~coloured ready~to~roll icing* ❋ *100 g (3½ oz) black ready~to~roll icing*
❋ *250 g (8 oz) royal icing sugar* ❋ *Black food colouring* ❋ *Icing sugar, for dusting* ❋ Makes 10

One: Use a palette knife to spread the cooled cupcakes with the buttercream.

Two: Dust your hands with icing sugar, take a 25 g (1 oz) ball of flesh-coloured icing and cut it in half. Flatten each half slightly and position on one of the cakes to form a bottom shape. Repeat with the remainder.

Three: Dust a work surface with icing sugar and thinly roll out the remaining icing. Cut out 10 discs using an 8 cm (3½ inch) cutter. Lay them over the cakes, smoothing to fit and eliminating any creases. Use a sharp knife to make a cut between the cheeks.

Four: Thinly roll out the black icing and cut out 10 skimpy knickers. Gently press onto the cakes, securing in place with a dampened paintbrush and trimming off any excess at the sides.

Five: Beat the royal icing sugar in a bowl with 5–6 teaspoons of water to make a smooth icing that only just holds its shape. Set aside one-quarter of the icing in a separate bowl and colour the remainder black. Spoon into a paper piping bag (see page 14) fitted with a writer nozzle and use to pipe suspenders and stocking tops onto the cakes.

Six: Put the reserved white icing in another piping bag fitted with a writer nozzle and pipe white lines along the suspenders and little flowers to finish.

Hey Suspender!

250 g (8 oz) royal icing sugar ✴ Pink, black and red food colourings ✴ 1 quantity White Chocolate Ganache (see page 13) ✴ 10 Vanilla Cupcakes (see page 8) ✴ Makes 10

One: Trace the outline of a pair of legs with high heeled shoes onto a piece of baking parchment. They should be roughly 7 cm (3 inches) long. For guidance use the photograph opposite, or refer to a book or the Internet to source your image.

Two: Put the royal icing sugar in a bowl and add enough water, about 6 teaspoons, to mix to a smooth paste. Beat in a dash of pink food colouring. Put a third of the icing in a paper piping bag (see page 14) and snip off the merest tip.

Three: Place another sheet of parchment over the outline. Pipe icing around the shape, then slide the top sheet of parchment along so you can pipe more legs. Add a few drops of water to the remaining icing, put in another piping bag with a larger hole and fill in the centres of the shapes. Leave to harden overnight.

Four: Place the chocolate ganache in a large paper piping bag fitted with a star-shaped nozzle and pipe swirls on the cakes.

Five: Use black and red food colourings and a fine paintbrush to paint suspenders, stockings and shoes onto the icing legs. Leave to dry, then press a pair of legs into the top of each cake.

Bunny Girl

1 quantity Amaretto Buttercream (see page 12) ✻ 10 Cherry Cupcakes (see page 8) ✻ 250 g (8 oz) royal icing sugar ✻ Black food colouring ✻ 100 g (3½ oz) pink ready~to~roll icing ✻ 200 g (7 oz) black ready~to~roll icing ✻ 25 g (1 oz) white ready~to~roll icing ✻ Icing sugar, for dusting ✻ Makes 10

One: Use a palette knife to spread buttercream on the cupcakes, making the surface as smooth as possible.

Two: Beat the royal icing sugar in a bowl with enough water, about 6 teaspoons, to make an icing that just holds its shape. Colour with black food colouring and put in a paper piping bag (see page 14), fitted with a writer nozzle. Alternatively, put in a paper piping bag and snip off the merest tip.

Three: Pipe parallel lines, about 5 mm (¼ inch) apart, over the cupcakes, then across in the opposite direction to give a 'fishnet' design. Reserve the remaining icing.

Four: Dust a work surface with icing sugar, roll out the pink icing and cut out lots of small bow ties. Secure around the edges of the cakes. You'll need 8–10 per cake.

Five: Cut the black icing into 10 equal pieces, dust your hands with icing sugar and mould each into a bunny costume. Insert a cocktail stick into the base of each and use to stick them on the cakes. Roll the white icing into 10 pea-sized balls and position one on each costume for a tail, securing in place with a dampened paintbrush. Use the remaining black piping icing to create the lacing down the backs of the bunny costumes.

Kinky Boots

250 g (8 oz) royal icing sugar ✻ Purple and black food colourings ✻ 10 Vanilla Cupcakes (see page 8) ✻ 1 quantity White Chocolate Ganache (see page 13) ✻ Makes 10

One: Trace the outline of a pair of thigh-high boots onto a piece of baking parchment. They should be roughly 7 cm (3 inches) long. For guidance use the photograph opposite, or refer to a book or the Internet to source your image.

Two: Put the royal icing sugar in a bowl and add enough water, about 6 teaspoons, to mix to a smooth paste. Reserve 3 tablespoons of the icing in a separate bowl and cover tightly. Beat purple food colouring into the remainder. Put a third of the purple icing in a paper piping bag (see page 14) and snip off the merest tip.

Three: Place another sheet of parchment over the boot outlines. Pipe icing around the edges of the shapes, then slide the top sheet of parchment along so you can pipe more boots. Add a few drops of water to the remaining purple icing, put in another piping bag with a larger hole and fill in the centres of the boots. Leave to harden overnight.

Four: Use a palette knife to spread the cooled cupcakes with the ganache. Gently press a pair of boots onto the ganache, supporting them at the back with a cocktail stick if necessary. Colour the remaining icing black and put in another piping bag, snipping off the merest tip. Use to decorate the boots and the edges of the cupcakes with tassels.

Down Boy

300 g (10 oz) black ready~to~roll icing ✱ 12 Rich Chocolate Cupcakes (see page 9) ✱ ½ quantity Dark Chocolate Ganache (see page 13) ✱ 200 g (7 oz) brown ready~to~roll icing ✱ 100 g (3½ oz) red ready~to~roll icing ✱ 6 m (20 ft) wired ribbon ✱ Icing sugar, for dusting ✱ Makes 12

One: Dust your hands with icing sugar and shape 15 g (½ oz) of black icing into a drum shape for a hat, then 5 g (¼ oz) into a disc for the brim. Secure together with a dampened paintbrush and transfer to a baking tray lined with baking parchment. Make 11 more in the same way.

Two: Roll a little more black icing into a rope about 2.5 mm (⅛ inch) wide, and cut into 3.5 cm (1½ inch) lengths for the whip handles. Transfer to the baking tray and leave for several hours to harden. Wrap and reserve the remaining black icing.

Three: Use a palette knife to spread the cooled cupcakes with ganache. Dust a work surface with icing sugar and roll out the brown icing thinly. Roll the red icing into very thin ropes, then lay them over the brown icing, spaced 1 cm (½ inch) apart. Gently roll with the rolling pin to make stripes. Cut out 12 discs using an 8 cm (3½ inch) cutter and lay over the cakes.

Four: Cut the ribbon into 12 lengths and tie around the cakes. Position the hats and whip handles on the cakes, securing with a dampened paintbrush. Roll the reserved black icing as thinly as possible under your fingers and arrange over the cakes in loops to make the whips.

Acknowledgements

Publisher: Sarah Ford
Managing Editor: Camilla Davis
Designer: Joanna MacGregor
Illustrator: Vanessa Bell
Food Stylist: Joanna Farrow
Photographer: Edward Allwright

Many of the cupcake cases were kindly
supplied by *Kalasform* who specialize in
decorative paper cupcake cases. Check
out their website www.kalasform.se or
look out for their products in specialist
cake decorating stores or through internet
mail order companies.